Albert Réville

The Song of Songs

Commonly called the Song of Solomon

Albert Réville

The Song of Songs
Commonly called the Song of Solomon

ISBN/EAN: 9783337175849

Printed in Europe, USA, Canada, Australia, Japan

Cover: Foto ©Thomas Meinert / pixelio.de

More available books at **www.hansebooks.com**

THE SONG OF SONGS,

COMMONLY CALLED

THE SONG OF SOLOMON,

OR,

THE CANTICLE.

FROM THE FRENCH OF

ALBERT RÉVILLE,

DOCTOR IN THEOLOGY,

PASTOR OF THE WALLOON CHURCH OF ROTTERDAM.

WILLIAMS AND NORGATE,
14, HENRIETTA STREET, COVENT GARDEN, LONDON;
AND 20, SOUTH FREDERICK STREET, EDINBURGH.
1873.

NOTE BY THE TRANSLATOR.

The following article which is now, with the permission of the Author, translated into English, first appeared in the *Revue de Théologie* of Strasbourg (1st Series, Vol. XIV.), and was afterwards published among the collected works of the Author. (See *Essais de Critique Religieuse, par Dr. Réville,* published by Joel Cherbuliez, Paris, *Nouvelle Edition,* 1869.)

In rendering the poem into English, the words of the ordinary English translation of the Bible have been used as far as applicable.

ERRATA.

Pages 1 and 37.—For " singing birds " read " songs."
Page 6.—Note.—For " Talmud " read " Targum."
Page 29.—Note.—For " portu " read " hortu."
Page 32, lines 8 and 11.—For " black " read " brown."
Page 49, line 10.—For " cannot " read " can only."

THE SONG OF SONGS.

I.

" Rise up, my love, my fair one, and come away,
For lo, the winter is past,
The rain is over and gone,
The flowers appear on the earth,
The time of the singing birds is come,
And the voice of the turtle is heard in our land."

. . . . . .

Such is a song of the spring-time, which a traveller along the western chain of the Lebanon, towards the end of the eighth century before our era, might have heard resounding among the pasturages of these green mountains. If he could foresee the future, and could have contemplated the destinies of the charming idyll, of which it forms part, his astonishment would have been great to see it transformed into a theological oracle, and furnishing a favourite theme of meditation to the most austere preachers of distant times. His astonishment would not be less if he could foresee the severity with which it might be treated by a posterity still more remote.

Nothing can be more extraordinary than the destiny of the book which we propose to study. On the one hand, reverenced as a casket of most precious mystical pearls, on the other hand accused of defiling the Bible by its presence; for some, a pure fountain of holy contemplation, for others a folly and a scandal; for the former, a limpid and wholesome spring, at which they might refresh their faith; for the latter an inexhaustible source of profane mockery; the book is at once surrounded with the glory of an aureola, and with the contempt of ignominy. Let us trace a sketch of its history.

It is placed in the canonical list of the sacred books of the Hebrews between Job and Ruth, and, consequently makes part of the collection of sacred writings or *hagiographs* which were added to the biblical collection subsequently to the prophetical and historical documents. As its claim to be entered in the canonical list, it may be presumed that it had, by that time, come to be considered as a work of King Solomon, and that its allegorical interpretation as such gave it a religious value to which in its origin it had little pretext. These two causes operated mutually, and were necessary to each other. Unless the book were ascribed to Solomon, it is not likely that it would have been received into the Canon, and except for its allegorical interpretation at the time when the Canon was fixed, it would not have been ascribed to Solomon.

One thing is certain, that the book soon came to occupy an eminent position in the rabbinical teaching. Jerome informs us that among the Jews it was not allowed to be read by persons under the age of thirty, not, as we might be inclined to think, on account of its dangers to the juvenile imagination, but on account of the theological profundities which it presented for contemplation, and which required the maturity of age to be adequately appreciated. The beginning of the book of Genesis, and the beginning and end of the book of Ezekiel, were for the same reason objects of the same precautions.* In the Talmud we find the eminent Rabbi Akiba expressing himself in these words:—"The whole world is not worth the day " on which the Canticle was given to Israel. All the " writings of the Canon are holy, but the Canticle is the " most holy of holies."† The same rabbi tells us that the only work of Solomon which has caused controversy is the Ecclesiastes.

However, the terms of the assertion of the Rabbi Akiba causes some suspicion that the unanimity as to the Canticle was not so absolute as he alleges, and in fact, in the same Talmudic treatise, we find Rabbi Jose state that the "Ecclesiastes does not defile the hands, " but that the Canticle is the subject of disputes."

In general, the Canticle when allegorized, becomes too easily the subject of those subtle interpretations to which the rabbinical school was so passionately addicted, in order to maintain prolonged argumentation. In such circumstances, reasons which otherwise would have tended to counteract belief in the Divine inspiration of the book, came to corroborate that belief. In

* Hieron. Op. Praef. ad Ezech.   † Mischna, Tract, Judaim. iii. 5.

—this way, a principle is formed and developed of which Christian theology has too long undergone the yoke. This principle may be formulated thus: the Bible is not a divine book because the contents of it are divine, but these contents are divine because they are in the Bible. In starting from such a principle, it was impossible not to allegorize the Canticle, and that result would come to predominate over every other feeling on the part of those who did so.

We fortunately find in the Jewish literature some traces of the allegorisation of the Canticle. In the book of the Wisdom of Solomon, ch. viii. 2, the author makes King Solomon, speaking of his wisdom, say, " I loved her and sought her out from my youth, " I desired to make her my spouse and I was a lover " of her beauty ;" and at ver. 18, " I went about seeking " how to take her to me." These words seem an echo of the allegorical interpretation of the Canticle. In that sense, the wisdom should be personified in the Shulamite, of whom King Solomon wished to gain the good graces. This, however, is merely a presumption. It is equally difficult to say what Philo, who certainly did not interpret literally, found in the Canticle. Josephus* ranks it among the last four books of the Jewish Bible, which he designates generally as " con- " taining the praises of God and rules of life for men." That definition implies that the Jewish historian also explained it allegorically.

It is remarkable that the New Testament, which so

* Cant. Apion. i. 8.

frequently quotes the Old Testament, is silent as regards the Canticle. I know that this assertion is disputed, and that some pretended references are brought forward against it which might as well shew that the writers of the New Testament have quoted Virgil or Theocritus. The only passage which, strictly speaking, offers any resemblance of the kind, is the description in the Epistle to the Ephesians (ch. v. 27) of the Church, considered as the mystic spouse of Christ, " a glorious church, not having spot or wrinkle or any " such thing." There is there some accordance with a passage of the Canticle (ch. iv. 7). But when it is considered with what facility the old Jewish idea, according to which the alliance between God and the chosen nation, was assimilated to a matrimonial contract, was adopted by the new Israel as the Church of the redeemed, it is impossible to imagine that there is any intentional resemblance between the two passages. The fact is, that the New Testament has in no way regarded or referred to a book which would have afforded powerful weapons for the time against the unbelieving Jews, if the interpretation which afterwards became traditional in the Christian Church, had then prevailed. It is not necessary to infer from that, as has sometimes been done, that the writers of the New Testament were prejudiced against the book or that they wished it to be forgotten. It is only permissible to conclude that their feelings, profoundly religious, were not much attracted by its contents. Perhaps also, the traditional Jewish interpretation which prevailed, and which was not then replaced by any parallel Christian interpretation, may have opposed itself indirectly to the use of the Canticle in the interest of the rising Church.

This Jewish interpretation, perpetuated under some differences of form, all along the traditions of the rabbins, consisted of regarding the Canticle as a figurative description of the mutual love between Jehovah and the chosen people. It was held to be a prediction of the final deliverance of Israel. We find that point of view developed in the Aramean Hierosolymite version, of which the unknown author lived shortly after the editing of the Talmud.* His interpretation may be considered as the type of all those which followed in the synagogue. It was in some sort refined by Aben Esdra, a Spanish Jew of the 12th century, who drew from it the whole history, past and future, of the Hebrew people, from Abraham downwards, and it was the rabbins who introduced the variations upon the fundamental theme. The philosopher Maimonides in his *More Nevochim*, alone proposed a special interpretation in the interest of his own mystico-pantheistic speculations. He holds the mention of kisses at the commencement of the book, to be a symbol to express the tendency to unity, of the Creator and of the creature.

Origen was, for the Christians, that which the Hierosolymite Targumist had been for the Jews, that is to say, he stereotyped in the Church the interpretation which became traditional. The mutual love between Christ and the Church is the essential *datum*. Atha-

* This Talmud is in the *Biblia Hebraica* of Buxtoff, printed at Basle, in 1618.

nasius departs considerably from the traditional type, in seeing in the Canticle a hymn in honour of the incarnation of the Eternal Word, *tanquam verbi et carnis epithalamium*. But the point of view of Origen continued to be master of the situation. However, Theodoret (5th century), an ardent defender of the allegorical interpretation of the poem, makes known to us several partisans of the literal interpretation. In the first rank of them shines Theodore of Mopspestia, whose resistance to the general opinion upon the Canticle, in which he saw nothing but descriptions of sensual love, drew upon him the condemnation of being a leader of heresy.

In the middle ages, the Canticle was a favourite book of the mystics. Bernard of Clairvaux and Bonaventure delighted in it. Remaining faithful to the general views of Origen, they introduced the new element of making it express the individual relations of the believer with Christ. It is no more limited to those of the Church with its Divine Head. Bernard justifies this by the principle that that which the whole possess, fully and integrally, the individuals have in part. The Abbot of Clairvaux composed eighty-six sermons on the Canticle. The most orthodox preacher of the present time could scarcely venture to do more.

Shortly before the Reformation, Nicolas de la Lyre[1] attempted to reconcile the Jewish interpretation with the Christian, by dividing the book into two parts, and in assigning for the subject of the first the history of Israel until the time of Jesus Christ, and for the second the history of the Church until the time of Constantine.

Luther, who detested allegory, and who dared not revert to the heretical view of Theodore of Mopsuestia, tried to clear a way for himself. But he could not prevent himself from lapsing into allegory. The Canticle was, according to him, a song of praises where Solomon thanked God for the gracious gift of the obedience of the people. It may be permitted to enquire if the excellent doctor was himself very well satisfied with his explanation. On that point, it suffices to see how he expresses himself, in his Latin Commentary, after having combated the allegorists:—"See then," says he, "in what manner I understand that book "touching the government of Solomon. If I deceive "myself, it is necessary to excuse a first attempt, for "the ideas of others are still very much more absurd."* That essay of Luther can never have any visible result upon general opinion.

In the Reformed Church the old interpretation was rigorously maintained, and in 1544, the Great Council of Geneva banished from the territory of the republic Sebast. Castalio (Chatillon), who had proposed, on his side, to banish from the Bible that curious book in which he could see nothing but a "conversation of "Solomon with a certain loving Shulamite."†

In the Romish Church the allegorical interpretation also preponderates, and the only phenomenon worthy of

---

* *Nam aliorum cogitationes longe plus absurditatis habent.*
† *Colloquium Salomonis cum amica quadam Sulamitha.*

remark, is that, very quietly, the Virgin Mary is substituted for the Church, under the traits of the betrothed of the Canticle. It is among the doctrines of Arminianism, that the first attempts of Protestant theology to obtain an historical and rational interpretation have arisen. Grotius* absolutely rejects all the allegories as untenable, and can see nothing more in the Canticle of Solomon, than a pleasant conjugal conversation, a *garritus conjugum inter se,* intermingled with songs. " The mys-" teries of marriage," says he, "are there disguised " under the pleasant envelope of language."† In his view the spouses were Solomon and the daughter of the King of Egypt, according to the first book of Kings, ch. iii. 1. The choirs were composed, probably, of young people attending near the nuptial chamber. The interpretation of Grotius may contain some gleams of truth, but in other respects it is detestable. The time when he lived, and the theological party of which he is the most illustrious representative, were altogether incapable of appreciating the poetic value and moral aspect of the book. In order to do so his time and his party would have required more elasticity of imagination, more aptitude to appropriate the ideas and manners of races which have long since disappeared, and more apprehension of the nature of popular poesy. In other words, they would have required that sense of antiquity which we have else-

* In his *Annotationes in Vet. Testament.*
† *Nuptiarum arcana sub honestis verborum involucris hic latent.*

where shewn to belong peculiarly to our own epoch. In fact, Grotius, in his explanations, renders the book more immoral than it is, and it is a remarkable spectacle to see that grave personage discover indecencies in the whole of it, and gross obscenities in texts which are perfectly innocent. He goes so far that we are unwilling to transcribe, even in Latin, the passages which justify the severity of our judgment. Grotius contributed, to a great extent, to confirm the reasoning which so long maintained the allegorical interpretation, after having given rise to it. The Canticle interpreted literally is immoral. If so, there is then an immoral book in the Bible. Such a conclusion is impious. It is therefore necessary, if its literal interpretation be immoral, to interpret it allegorically. The Voltairian unbelief was enchanted at coming into contact with such a delightful confusion of reasoning. It was in a great measure owing to the unsatisfactory impression produced by the explanation of Grotius, that J. Cocceius, the great Protestant allegorist, owed the success of his Commentary, where, going beyond the previous allegories, he transforms the Canticle into an Apocalypse, finding in it the entire history of the Church, from its origin till the final judgment, and finding, in the end of the seventh chapter, a prediction of the Reformation. That work, the author of which mentions that he was guided in his divinations by the Holy Spirit, agreed so well with the opinions of the epoch at which it was produced,—an epoch at which orthodoxy, arrived at its apogee, regarded with instinctive mistrust the appearance of anything like criticism—that notwithstanding the controversies, then very animated, between the Lutherans and other Reformers, the views of Cocceius were adopted in both camps. About the end of the 17th century, Heunich, the Lutheran writer, known by his apocalyptic calculations, naturalized these views in his Church.

In the first half of the 18th century, Leclerc, who was an Arminian, like Grotius, and who was a worthy successor to him, as regards both his extensive learning and his æsthetic incapacity, saw in the Canticle an idyll altogether terrestrial, in which Solomon disguised as a shepherd (!) amuses himself with one of his wives or concubines, perhaps the daughter of Pharaoh. He had for his principal antagonist, against these views, F. G. Carpsovius,* who was obliged to urge, in support of the traditional explanation of the book, "the espousal " of Christ with the Church and the redeemed." But the flow of opinion was no longer so favourable to that view as at the time of Cocceius. Michaelis delivered a great blow against the traditional interpretation,† in declaring himself opposed to it, and he was the first who propounded the true view that the book, interpreted naturally, was far from deserving its evil reputation, since the love it depicted was "chaste conjugal " love." J. C. Jacobi, a clergyman of Celle, in 1771, took a decided part on behalf of the morality of the Canticle, and although he was sufficiently unfortunate

* *Introd. ad libros Canon. N. et V. Testam.* 1757.
† In his *Praelectiones de sacra poesi Hebraeorum*, 1770.

in the romance which he invented, in order to explain it, he discovered many points which modern researches have subsequently confirmed. For example, he demonstrated that Solomon could not be the author of a book in which he played a part very little flattering to his own self-esteem, and he also said that the book treated of a chaste affection, which the king attempted to divert from its legitimate object.* That work made some sensation, since the learned jurist Puffendorf took in hand to controvert it,† and to sustain the typical interpretation so much endangered. He believed himself able to strengthen that interpretation by invoking a pretended hieroglyphic tongue borrowed by Solomon from Egypt, and serving as an envelope to the esoteric doctrines of the Israelitish king. That was another romance.

Herder, who, of all the writers of the 18th century, best understood the poetry of the Bible, came, at length, to put in view the admirable beauty of a book so long obscured by empty divinations on the one hand, and unsuitable explanations on the other. He developed his ideas on the Canticle in his book, *Lieder der Liebe, die aeltesten und schoensten aus dem Morgenlande*, 1778. He, at least, felt how much there was of real and ingenuous chastity in those descriptions, of which it was maintained that the literal sense polluted the Bible. Although Herder may be completely mistaken in regard to the composition of the Canticle, of

---

* Das von seinen Worwürfen gerettete Hohelied, 1771.
† Unschreibung des Hohenliedes, 1776.

which he does not perceive the unity, and although he divides it, as Richard Simon does, into several distinct idyllic songs, he has the merit of raising the views of the interpreters who came after him to the proper elevation of sentiment, without which it is impossible to understand such a book.

The German critics, since the commencement of the present century, have followed Herder in the views put forward by him, but unequally and with infinitely less æsthetic tact. The rationalistic school has more than once relapsed into platitude, in the moralities which they have sought to draw from the Canticle. However, the allegorical interpretation was altogether fallen into disuse, even among the orthodox ranks, and it caused great surprise to see Rosenmuller attempt to revive it. He supported his views upon the recent discovery of several Indian and Persian productions, of which the sense was allegorical, and which presented certain analogies with the Hebrew Canticle. But he forgot to enquire whether or not the allegory was not, for them as for it, an arbitrary explanation.

The Roman Catholic theologian Hug* also allegorises the Canticle, but in a manner entirely novel. According to him it treats of the ten tribes personified in the Shulamite, and of King Hezekiah, represented by Solomon. Israel, upon the ruins of Samaria, sighs after her re-union with Judah, and King Hezekiah desires to accomplish it. This is one of those numerous

* Das Hohelied, 1813.

attempts at intermediate criticism, of which the worthy professor of Friburg was so affluent, and by means of which he hoped to fill up the continually increasing abyss between independent science and the traditions of his Church. Resumed by Kaiser in 1835, that hypothesis soon succumbed under the innumerable objections which it provoked.

We come at length to the works which have given to modern science the natural explanation, and which have impressed themselves, by their own evidence, upon all unprejudiced minds. Ammon, in 1780, had surmised the truth, but, since his time, two writers of very different tendencies from him, have brought it fully to light. M. Umbreit, whose orthodox reputation ought to free him from any imputation of heresy,* and M. Ewald, the most learned man of our time in the history of the Hebrew people,† have concurred in recognizing the unity of the composition of the book, and the irrefutable characteristics of a dialogue, implying a history, which can be reconstructed according to the indications which are given. There was therefore a dramatic element in the poem, and it was not impossible to re-establish its sense and action by judicious interpretation. That idea, received at first with some disfavour, at length made way, and has now obtained almost a unanimity of competent suffrages. M. M.

---

* Lied der Liebe das aelteste und schoenste aus dem Morgenlande. Goettingen, 1820.

† Erkloerung des Hohenliedes, 1826.

Boettger,* Loszner,† Hirzel,‡ and more recently M. M. E. Meier§ of Tubingen, and Hitzig|| of Zurich, have adopted, confirmed, and developed it. In Holland it has obtained the assent of two distinguished theologians, M. M. Veth and Hoekstra, and we may add, from personal knowledge, that of the learned professor of Leyden, M. Kuenen. M. Veth, Professor of Oriental languages at Amsterdam, has consecrated to the Canticle an excellent article in the Bybelsh Woerdenboek (published at Amsterdam since 1852), a sort of explanatory encyclopædia of the Bible, to which contributions have been made by a great number of learned Dutchmen. M. Hoekstra, Professor at the Baptist seminary in the same city, has made the book the subject of a very elaborate work, which was first inserted in the *Jaarboeken voor wetenschap, Theologie,* (Utrecht, 1855, pp. 323-468), and which has since been separately published.¶ This work, which is recommended by the scrupulous care of its details, and the philological erudition of its country, equally corroborates the interpretation which we propose to submit to the judgment of our readers. We have also been surprised and gratified to find it equally adopted by the authors of a colossal English Introduction to the Books of

* Exegetisch-kritische, Æhrenlese. Leipsic, 1849.
† German translation of Canticle, Salomo und Sulamith, 1851.
‡ Das Lied der Lieder. Zurich, 1840.
§ Das Hohelied, Tubingen, 1854, and in the Geschichte der poet. National-Literatur der Hebraer. Liepsic, 1856.
|| Das Hohelied erkloert, 1855.
¶ De triumph der Liefde in alle Beproeving. Utrecht, 1856.

the Bible, which appeared in 1856, in four large volumes.* It may be said of these results of independent criticism of this book, as of the interpretation now fixed for the Apocalypse, that to demonstrate it, it is sufficient to state it.

As might be expected, the re-actionary school, of which M. Hengstenberg has long been the leading oracle, has made numerous attempts to repel an explanation which, in absolving the Canticle from the accusations of irreligious unbelief, is incompatible with the idea of a Bible dictated throughout, from beginning to end, by the Holy Spirit. But their efforts have merely gone to shew their position to be untenable. Whilst M. Hengstenberg, followed by M. M. Keil and O. de Gerlach, replace in honour the old allegory of Christ and of the Church (1827 and 1853), one M. Golz, returns to the theory of Cocceius, and transforms the Canticle into an apocalypse, in which the Church can read her final destinies. It is unnecessary to add, that he finds in it clear and certain signs of the approaching end of the world.† Such is always the result of apocalyptic calculations. In the ranks of the reaction, M. Delitzsch is the writer who has made the greatest concession to independent criticism, but he has endeavoured to withdraw himself

---

* Introduction to the Critical Study and Knowledge of the Holy Scriptures, by the Rev. T. Hartwell Horne, revised and brought down to the present time by the Rev. Hartwell Horne, Rev. Samuel Davidson, and S. P. Tregelles. London, 1856.

† Hohelied Salomo's, 1850.

from the natural consequences of his concessions, by offering an explanation peculiar to himself.* Rejecting as untenable the traditional allegory, recognizing the unity, and even the dramatic character of the poem, he maintains that Solomon, in the Canticle, has simply intended to depict the mysteries of marriage in their most exclusive and endearing relations. But if the King of Israel thought and spoke licentiously, the Holy Spirit may have wished that in these erotic poems the people of God, returned from captivity, and the Church in her mystical communion with Christ, should find in later times, their holy aspirations retraced. For the natural marriage is in itself mysterious and a type of communion with God. It may be said, without fear, that such an explanation as this is equivalent to an avowal of defeat. It is true, then, that in itself, and in the mind of its author, the subjects of the Canticle are terrestrial. It is true then, that in order to interpret it, it is necessary to disengage the mind of all allegorical prepossessions. That being settled, it remains for consideration whether or not a biblical book, or any other book, can be meant to say any other thing than that which it says. We may mention, in the last place, the equally unfortunate attempt of H. A. Hahn,† who sees in the Canticle a prediction of the victory obtained over the heathen, by the love of Israel, and who finds the conversion of the negroes, in what is

* Das Hohelied untersucht und ausgelegt, 1851.
† Das Hohelied von Salomo, 1852.

C

said of the "little sister" of the Shulamite, in ch. viii. 8. Such an example of these extravagances, demonstrates better than anything else how far the traditional view is untenable.

We do not stop to refute it. Perhaps too many of its partizans have never taken the trouble to examine in detail, the consequences which follow from any attempt to apply it to the text of the book. They have too readily said that it depicts in a figurative manner the mystical union of Christ and of the Church. But when one puts himself in that view to follow the text, word by word, he must be singularly embarrassed. There are some passages which are perfectly opposed to it. It would be easy to excite a smile by giving some specimens of the ridiculous interpretations to which such a system would lead. We renounce willingly any success of this kind. We content ourselves, in all confidence, with such reasoning as may apply to our religious and moral sense.

The motive which has led, and continues to lead religious people to allegorise the Canticle, is simply that if it be necessary to ascribe to it its natural signification, there would be an immoral book in the Bible. If so, it would be necessary to admit that the Holy Spirit of God employs an immoral medium to address our souls! to express the purest emotions! to incarnate in us the most august mysteries! We recoil in horror from such a consequence.

I hasten now to add that the Canticle, interpreted naturally, can not lend itself in the least degree to allegory, but, on the other hand, it is very far from constituting an immoral book in its general conception. If, as regards our modern manners, it inevitably contains some indelicate passages, that is an inconvenience which is unavoidable, in putting ourselves into community of ideas with Oriental antiquity ; but, making this allowance, the fundamental intention of the poem is profoundly moral and beautiful. Would to God that the great part of our popular poetry on the same passion might contain the same teaching.

II.

We hope that we shall not be misunderstood in regard to the kind of evidence which we bring forward in favour of the interpretation which we are about to propound. That interpretation is not intended to be an illumination *a giorno* of the entire book, throwing light upon the most minute details. All who have studied the literature of antiquity know well that they may be able to perceive perfectly the general characteristics and principal ideas of a book, without being able to unravel all the obscurities. The general perspective, under which the poem should be considered, we believe to be certain, and that is the only conviction which we seek to impress. It is for that reason that we do not impose on our readers any discussions which might divert their attention. Those among them who may wish to know the details can find ample exposition of them in the works which we have cited. The work which we now submit to them, as we humbly avow, is an eclectic production, and owes its whole merit, if it has merit, to the views of others. It is not but here and there that we have followed our own course, but we attach so much the less importance to these independent excursions, that, after each of them, we always return to the road which has been already cleared for us by numerous and able pioneers.

The Song of Songs is a lyrical and pastoral poem, containing dramatic action, and having for its subject the victory of chaste and faithful love over the seductions of a king, whose passion, without being precisely illegitimate in the age and country into which it carries us, has nevertheless licentiousness for its motive. This is the story which the poem discloses throughout. If astonishment or doubt be excited by this view, we pray the reader to suspend his judgment until after the perusal of the references we are immediately about to make to the book itself.

King Solomon, whose pomp-loving and polygamous tastes are well known, finds himself in the tribe of Issachar at Baal-hamon, not far from Carmel, (chap. viii. 11.) and in the neighbourhood of a village of which the name is written Shunem,* but which the people commonly call Sulem or Sulam. There is still pointed out to travellers a hamlet situated about the same place which the Arabs name Solam.† It was there that they

---

* Josh. xix. 18.　1 Sam. xxviii. 4.　2 Kings iv. 8.
† Robinson's Palestine, iii. p. 402.

went to seek the fair damsel Abishag,* whose radiant youth cherished the last days of David "when he was "well stricken in years, and gat no heat." That country appears to have been renowned then for the beauty of its women. It is, accordingly, a young and fair Shulamite, who, without being aware, went alone too near to the Royal encampment, and whom the attendants of Solomon carried off and brought to him as worthy to enter his harem. But the girl had been betrothed by her mother to a shepherd in the neighbourhood, and the warm affection of both of them accompanied their engagement. Solomon became strongly enamoured of the fair peasant, but all his attempts to seduce her from her fidelity to her betrothed were foiled. It is in vain, that, in order to induce her to espouse him, he addresses to her the most flattering compliments, in vain that he displays before her all the magnificence of his Court, in vain even that he offers her the first place among his numerous wives. The girl remains firm, and, in a series of songs, which respond to the advances of the King, she finishes by convincing him of their inutility. It is in the contest between the fidelity which is inspired by true love and the allurements of flattered vanity, that the interest of the drama consists. We learn little by little, in listening to the songs of the Shulamite, to know her story and her feelings, as well as the circumstances which preceded her being carried away. On a spring day, early in

* 1 Kings i. 3-15.

the morning, her betrothed had come to her and engaged her to go out with him, that they might enjoy together the flowers and the perfumes and the singing of the birds, (chap. ii. 8-14). But her brothers, who, on two occasions in the poem, appear as the stern guardians of the honour of the family,* and seem to take the place of their deceased father, do not approve of that kind of useless promenade, and ordered their sister to go and watch the vineyard with the other people of the house. This results from the comparison of chap. i. 5, with chap. ii. 15.

>Chase us the foxes,
>The little foxes,
>That spoil the vineyards, &c.

Separated from her lover, the girl thinks of the time when she shall be re-united to him, and, occupied with her thoughts, leaves the vineyard and ventures beyond it, (ch. ii. 16, and ch. vi. 11, 12). It was then that she was carried away. Almost all the songs of the Shulamite are dedicated to describe the ceaseless and unalterable firmness of the love which she and her betrothed have vowed to each other. At the same time, she takes care to make the daughters of Jerusalem, who hear her and put occasional questions to her, understand that her love, which is so ardent, is free from all reproach. At a given moment (ch. iii. 6) the place of the scene changes, and we are brought to Jerusalem, where we assist at the triumphal cortege of Solomon, who wishes to celebrate his

* Comp. Genesis, ch. xxxiv.

espousals with his new favourite. For he did not yet despair of obtaining her good graces. But, as we have already mentioned, his solicitations were useless, and tired of his efforts, he sent back the girl to her relations and her betrothed, and we find her, at the end of the poem, enjoying the merited felicity of her chaste victory. Solomon, even although *not* viewed according to the ideas of modern civilization, does not perform a very distinguished part in all this. However, his final decision is an act of wisdom, and perhaps also of good policy in regard to a country which, like the North of Palestine, might not have supported indefinitely the excesses of despotism.

The fundamental idea of the poem is then that which is expressed by the heroine herself, (ch. viii. 6, &c) :—

> Love is strong as death,
> Jealousy is cruel as the grave,

(or, ardent affection is unyielding as the grave),

> The flames thereof are flames of fire,
> Of the lightnings of Jehovah.

We find the same idea in several places, in the course of the book, formulated in the conjuration, or sort of refrain, which the Shulamite addresses to the daughters of Jerusalem, who exhort her to accept the offers of the King—

> I conjure you, daughters of Jerusalem,
> By the roes, and by the hinds of the field,
> That ye stir not up, nor provoke love,
> Before the heart so inclines.

We have spoken of the lyrical and dramatic elements which mingle in the poem. In reality the Canticle is, at the same time, a song and a drama, and one of the questions raised by the contemporary interpreters, who have recognized the general sense of the book, is to know in which category it should be ranked. It seems to us that the two opinions, those which refuse to recognize it as a drama, and those which maintain it to be one, have each a part of the truth. If, by a drama is to be understood action represented according to the recognized laws of the Greek or modern drama, evidently the Canticle is not a drama. Occasionally, and in the same scene, unity of place is observed, as in the old engravings, where, in the foreground, Joseph explains to the chief baker his sinister dream, and in the distance he is, at the same time, already seen hung on the gallows. But it cannot be denied that the dialogue describes a contest of sentiment and passions, that it refers to facts which lead to that contest, and that it terminates in a real *denouement*. On the one hand, the Canticle can very well be sung by a single voice, as our popular ballads, in which so frequently several persons are made to speak, without their entering or leaving being marked otherwise than by the sense of the words. On the other hand, through the complaisance of imagination, which children and childish people put willingly at the service of whatever amuses them, the Canticle can very well be held as its own performance. In a word, the Canticle holds the place between the minstrel's lay, and the mystery of the middle ages, and if we express, at all hazards, the modern *genus* which it resembles most, we would indicate the *opera*. Is an opera exclusively a drama? Does it not also enter the field of lyric poetry, and sacrifice every instant the essential conditions of the drama to the exigencies of the song? Well! the lay of the Hebrew troubadour is found in analogous conditions, he sings a dialogue containing dramatic action.

This idea of its being a drama has brought against the modern explanation of the Canticle, its most able adversaries. It was formerly admitted, without dispute, that all dramatic forms were foreign to the Hebrew mind. This view was maintained from the complete absence, from the literature of the Bible, of the traces of any drama whatever, and this absence was ascribed to the innate estrangement of the Semitic races from everything of the nature of plastic art. Now, the drama may be called the plastic art of literature. The narrative and its teaching, or the moral in the drama, take a visible shape, and become, as it were, graven images. The Hebrew sings, teaches, prays in his poems, but he does not represent; the lyrical and didactic genius, the spontaneous description of sentiment which impels the poet, or doctrine presented under a poetic clothing, which renders it more impressive and popular, such are the forms natural to that people, to which we owe the Psalms, the heroic songs, the prophecies, the book of Job, the Proverbs, but which has left neither epopee nor dramas.

Otherwise, the members of the Semitic races cannot divest themselves of their individuality, to identify themselves with passions which are not their own, and that is evidently the fundamental condition of dramatic composition.

All these remarks were very ingenious. I even believe that to a considerable extent they are founded on the truth. But what then? If the Canticle, without being a drama in all the force of the term, contains very real dramatic elements, is it not necessary that theory yield to fact, and to admit that the Semitic mind is not so entirely opposed to the drama as they would wish to make it?

Is it legitimate to deduce consequences so absolute from the general character of a race or of a people? The French do not possess the genius of epic poetry, but does it follow that their literature has never produced anything resembling an epopee? Speaking generally, the theories of history, which are now made so successfully, upon natural tendencies, must involve occasional exceptions to their absolute truth. Thus, the Semitic races are undoubtedly monotheistic in their general tendency, and yet both idolatry and polytheism have been very frequent among them. How, then, do we still maintain the tendency of the Semitic races to be monotheistic? We do so because the monotheism of the world is their work; it is by that they have made their position in history, it is by that their illustrious men have been distinguished. The Semitic races are monotheistic in the same sense as the Greek races are artistic. Yet the latter included the brutish Spartans and the clownish Boetians. In the same way the Semitic Canaanites and Babylonians participated in the most hideous religions of the ancient world. But the fact that a race or a people have a general tendency is no proof that circumstances at variance with such a tendency may not be occasionally found in their history.

I say then, that while I accord to historians all that they put forward in regard to the aversion to dramatic conception in the Hebrew mind, I reserve the right, nevertheless, to establish exceptions to that general rule, when facts constrain me to do so. Is it however quite certain that that aversion was so profound? Is not symbolism, going sometimes even the length of mimicry, indigenous with the Semitic races? Does it not occasionally furnish to the prophets, the *élite* of these races, some forms of strange energy and remarkable frequency? Is the interval wide between developed symbolism, and the drama? Cannot it be said that there are dramatic elements in the book of Job? Even if the drama were completely foreign to the scope of the Hebrew mind, and if it were difficult to conceive the composition of the Canticle in the kingdom of Judah, there may not be the same difficulty in regard to a remote fraction of the people of Israel, placed beyond the circumference of the Hebraic circle. Now the Canticle, as we shall afterwards see, belongs in its origin to the north of Palestine, to a district in frequent contact with the caravans from Tyre, and where the pure Hebrew type might probably begin to lose its more rigid characteristics.

It remains to make very large allowance for the profound differences of manners, of time, and of place. If the Canticle involves the idea of the drama, it nowhere does that of the theatre; and some of its modern interpreters have prejudiced their explanations, by attempting to adapt it to our dramatic divisions of acts and scenes. I can easily picture to my mind the Canticle sung among the village population of an oriental scene and climate, assembled in the evening near one of their fountains, to refresh and amuse themselves. Two or three sweet voices to sing the principal parts, a choir to give the answers, and easily able to perform several parts successively (without counting that of spectators), was all that was necessary to its representation, if it was represented, as to which I make no assertion. I may add, however, that the Canticle might have some relation to the *Asamer*, or songs intermingled with dances, which Burckhardt has heard among the Bedouins of Mount Sinai. It is in the evenings that the young people of the tribe gather together for these diversions.* It is necessary to remember that the customs of the Arabs allow much more freedom to women than those of the Turks or Persians. In this respect, as in many others, they approach much more nearly to those of the Hebrews.

* That is the opinion of M. E. Meier (Gesch. der nat. poet. Lit. der Hebraer, p. 73 *et seq.*), and we find in the Canticle itself several traits which confirm it.

In order to appreciate the poetry of the Canticle it is necessary to keep in view that we must expect to find in it a sort of imagery which, to modern European taste, must appear extremely strange and unsuitable. It is every where full of comparisons which justify this assertion. The characteristic of its figurative language is that the image borrows its application, much less from any external resemblance in form or colour of the objects compared, than from the analogy of the subjective impressions caused by these objects. Thus, the nose of the Shulamite is compared to the " Tower " of Lebanon which looketh towards Damascus." That comparison, so strange to us, has for its *medium* the sentiment of its subject being gracefully placed in the midst of objects agreeable to the view. In the same manner, the Shulamite compares the lips of her lover to lilies.* Another local characteristic of the poetic language is, that the points of comparison the most appreciated, relate to the objects which were held in the highest estimation, according to the tastes and manners of the country. The fresh and sparkling

* This kind of comparison, especially in erotic poetry, would have been less surprising to the Western Greek and Roman than to us. M. Hoekstra has found, in Ovid and Anacreon, various passages resembling those of the Canticle. The former, for example, addresses to Galatea such compliments as these : " *Riguo formosior portu, platano conspectior alba, nobilior pomis, matura dulcior uva,*" &c. There is an almost incredible comparison of a young girl, who is complimented, to a horse (l. 9), which we also find in Theocritus, xviii. 30.

η αρματι Θεσσαλος ιππος
Ωδε και α-ροδοχρως Ελενα Λακιδαιμονι κοσμος.

rills, the precious stones, and above all the perfumes, —a source of physical enjoyment to which the Orientals are certainly more sensible than we are—present themselves every moment to the imagination of the popular singer. Besides this, it should not occasion surprise, if the responses of the interlocutors are rarely direct, and leave their real meaning rather to be implied than expressed positively. This, again, is altogether characteristic of the East, and of a country where they answer the most pressing questions by a similitude or an enigma.

We hope, from what we have stated, to have sufficiently prepared our readers for what is to follow. They ought to appreciate the degree of evidence and the nature of the difficulties of which the version we proceed to give is susceptible. Supposing that the words of a modern opera were to come into the hands of a very remote posterity, to whom our language shall be a dead one, and that nothing should distinctly indicate to the readers of that period, the division of the scenes, and the succession of the personages, any one who might attempt, from the indications furnished by the words so preserved, to re-establish the primitive divisions, would have a task similar to that which we have tried to accomplish. So far, it would be easy to him, if certain that it was a dialogue he had before him, to design, with some assurance, the fundamental idea, and the principal elements of the action, so far he might get beyond mental hesitation, as to the soundness of the division which he might so re-establish, but while the evidence might sustain the general result there might perhaps remain great obscurity on many points of detail.

III.

We repeat that it would be contrary to the spirit of the time and of the poem to apply our dramatic divisions to it. But there are in it some scenes, some *tableaux*, which arise successively in the imagination of the poet, and we use them as a natural and easy mode of dividing the poem.

Scene I. On the occasion at which the song commences, the Shulamite is brought into the midst of a group of women of the harem, who have been desired to influence her in favour of the advances of Solomon. Her own thoughts are occupied entirely with her love for her betrothed, whom she calls for in vain. She speaks to him as if he was present, her whole soul belongs to him. Then, with a vivacity altogether feminine, she questions the women who examine her curiously, while she is eulogising his beauty. She is in despair at having failed to guard her vineyard, that is to say her betrothed. That and other analogous comparisons recur frequently in the poem.

THE SHULAMITE.

I. 2. Let him kiss me with the kisses of his mouth,
  For thy love is better than wine.
 3. Because of the savour of thy good ointments,
  Thy name is like ointment poured forth,
  Therefore do the virgins love thee.

4. Draw me after thee, let us go away,
   The king brings me into his chambers.

CHORUS OF WOMEN.

Let us be glad and rejoice in thee,
Let us remember thy love more than wine,
The upright love thee.

THE SHULAMITE.

5. I am black, but comely, O, daughters of Jerusalem,
   As the tents of Kedar,*
   As the curtains of Solomon.
6. Look not upon me, if I am black,
   It is because the sun hath looked on me;
   My mother's children were angry with me,
   They made me keeper of the vineyards,
   But mine own vineyard have I not kept.
7. Tell me, oh, thou whom my soul loveth,
   Where thou feedest thy flock,
   Where thou restest at noon,
   For why should I be wandering
   Towards the flocks of thy companions.

The women are astonished, and perhaps feel a certain contempt for a peasant who despises honours, which seem to them to surpass all the dreams of feminine ambition, and say to her ironically;

---

* Kedar was a nomad Ishmaelite people who wandered about the north-east of Palestine, and whose tents, shining in the sun, from time to time appeared in the distance to the eyes of the mountaineers of the Lebanon.

8. Since thou art not reasonable,
   O thou fairest among women,
   Follow then the footsteps of the flock,
   And feed thy kids
   Beside the tents of the shepherds.

Scene II. The royal lover appears, and commences by praising the beauties of the Shulamite, and speaks to her of the rich adornments which will make her still more beautiful. He never imagines that his advances can be repelled. But the young girl answers to him that she is entirely absorbed with thoughts of her betrothed. That thought is the spikenard* which exhales its perfume continually, even before the king arrives. Solomon redoubles his flatteries. The Shulamite falls back upon the thought of her lover, and indirectly refuses the offers of the king, in preferring the beauties of her native country, in the midst of which, flower of the field as she is herself, she is more in her place and more happy than in the midst of the pomps of the Court. The first conversation of Solomon with the young captive terminates by a vigorous description of the passionate love which inspires her for her betrothed, followed by the conjuration to the daughters of Jerusalem, of which we have already spoken.

* Spikenard is an Indian perfume, which in ancient times was very highly esteemed. Compare Mark xiv. 3-5.

SOLOMON.

9. I have compared thee, O my love,
   To my horse in the chariot of Pharaoh,*
10. Thy cheeks are comely with collars of pearls,
    And thy neck with chains of coral.
11. We shall make thee chains of gold,
    With studs of silver.

THE SHULAMITE.

12. While the king sitteth at his table,
    My spikenard sendeth forth the smell thereof,
13. For a bundle of myrrh is my well beloved,
    He shall lie all night upon my bosom,
14. My beloved is unto me as a cluster of camphire
    In the vineyards of Engedi.†

SOLOMON.

15. Behold thou art fair, my love,
    Behold thou art fair,
    Thou hast dove's eyes.

THE SHULAMITE.

16. Behold thou art fair, my beloved, yea, pleasant,
    Also, our bed is green.‡

---

* That is to say, before a fine chariot of Egypt. This comparison makes allusion, not less to the richness of the harness, than to the grace of the animal. In the *Asamer* the young Arabs compare the objects of their addresses to camels, their favourite animal.

† Engedi was a locality in the south of Palestine, renowned for its gardens, and, according to Josephus (Antiq. ix. 1), fertile in balsam and palm trees.

‡ The young girl applies to her lover the compliments which the king makes to her. She makes allusion at the same time to the simplicity of their condition.

SOLOMON.

17. The beams of our house are cedar,
And our rafters (or pannelling) of fir.*

THE SHULAMITE.

II. 1. I am a simple rose of Sharon,†
A lily of the valleys.

SOLOMON.

2. As a lily among thorns,
So is my love among girls.

THE SHULAMITE.

3. As the apple tree‡ among the trees of the wood,
So is my beloved among young men,
I loved to seat myself under his shadow,
His fruit was sweet in my mouth.

---

* Solomon connects with the last words of the Shulamite the eulogy of the palace which he will give her to reside in. Compare with this what the first Book of Kings tells us as to the houses built by Solomon. Ch. v. and vii.

† Sharon designates a flowery district, which extends from the foot of Carmel, and slopes gently towards the Mediterranean. Compare Isaiah, ch. xxxiii. 9, and xxxv. 2. It is impossible for us to translate the proper name of the flower to which the Shulamite compares herself. There is no means of giving its scientific name, *colchicum*, and still less its popular name, *tue-chien*, or *safran-batard*. It is an autumnal plant with violet flowers, and abounds among the grass of the plains. The Germans call it the *Zeitlose*. In the Dutch M. Hoekstra is puzzled by the same difficulty, and prefers to cut the knot, as we do, rather than apply, as figurative of the Shulamite, the horrible word *Herfsttydeloose*.

‡ The apple trees of Syria are a very large species, and their fruits are remarkable for their good odour. See Winer, Realwoert, b. art. Apfelbaum.

4. He brought me into the banquetting house,*
   And his banner over me was love.
5. Stay me with flagons,†
   Comfort me with the perfumes of apples,
   For I am sick of love.
6. That his left hand may be under my head,
   That his right hand may embrace me.
7. I conjure you, daughters of Jerusalem,
   By the roes, and by the hinds of the field,
   That ye stir not up, nor provoke love,
   Before the heart so inclines.

After having thus expressed the vivacity of her attachment for her betrothed, attachment which, we shall soon see, was much more chaste than these expressions appear in the first instance to infer, the Shulamite relates two scenes of her previous life, which form the subject of the two solos which follow. If we venture to pursue our comparison of the Canticle with a modern opera, we should call these two *cavatinas* two romances, destined to explain circumstances or sentiments which cannot find place in the dialogue.

In the first song the girl depicts the profound love of her betrothed for her, and at the same time recalls

---

* Literally, *He makes me to enter into the cellar, where they guard the wine,* that is say, that he rejoices my heart as if there were an assemblage in such a place.

† That is to say, send me to my betrothed, whom she has compared to a vine, ch. i. 6, in the same manner as she has just compared him to an apple tree.

the occasion from which her misfortunes proceeded, the order which her brothers gave her to go to guard the vineyard. The song of the brothers, analogous to that which we find further on, ch. viii. 8, with its rudeness and its positive character, breaks in, in a manner very original, upon the charming warbling of love which precedes, and which truly touches the sweetest notes of bucolic sentiment. While the betrothed lovers see in the spring time but the accord of nature with their young loves, the brothers turn their attention to the work which the season renders necessary.

FIRST SONG OF THE SHULAMITE.

II. 8. The voice of my beloved,
Behold! he cometh leaping upon the mountains,
Skipping upon the hills.
9. My beloved is like a roe, or a young hart,
Behold! he standeth behind our wall,
He looketh forth at the windows,
He sheweth himself thro' the lattice.
10. My beloved spake, and said to me,
Rise up, my love, my fair one, and come away,
For lo, the winter is past,
The rain is over and gone,
12. The flowers appear on the earth,
The time of the singing birds is come,
And the voice of the turtle is heard in our land,

13. The fig tree putteth forth her green figs,
    The vines with the tender grape give a good smell,
    Arise, my love, my fair one, and come away.
14. O my dove that art in the clefts of the rock,
    In the secret places of their steps,
    Let me see thy countenance,
    Let me hear thy voice,
    For sweet is thy voice,
    And thy countenance is comely.

But in place of the clear notes of the girl, it is the rough voice of her brothers which makes itself to be heard.

THE BROTHERS.

15. Chase us the foxes,
    The little foxes,
    That spoil the vineyards,
    For our vines have tender grapes.

THE SHULAMITE.

16. My beloved is mine,
    And I am his,
    He pastures his flock among the lilies.
17. Before the day break,
    Before the shadows flee away.
    Return, my beloved,
    Like a roe or a young hart,
    Upon the hills which are furrowed by the valleys.

The second song has for its object to depict the affection of the girl for him whom her soul loveth, but more especially to make it to be understood that her conduct is pure, and that her love has been legitimated by the consent of her mother. This song is again terminated by the conjuration already given.

SECOND SONG OF THE SHULAMITE.

III. 1. By night on my bed I sought
  Him whom my soul loveth—
  I sought him, but I found him not.
  2. I will rise now, and go about the town,
  In the streets and in the broad ways,
  I will seek him whom my soul loveth,
  I sought him, but I found him not.
  3. I found the watchmen that go about the town
  Saw you him whom my soul loveth?
  4. It was but little that I passed from them,
  When I found him whom my soul loveth,
  I held him and would not let him go,
  Till I brought him into my mother's house,
  Into the chamber of her that bare me.
  5. I conjure you, daughters of Jerusalem,
  By the roes, and by the hinds of the field,
  That ye stir not up, nor provoke love,
  Before the heart so inclines.

Scene III. In the mind of the Hebrew troubadour the locality of the scene has evidently changed. We assist at a triumphal *cortege* presided over by King

Solomon, who celebrates new espousals. The chorus is held to express the admiration of the spectators of the procession. Each mentions the object which makes the strongest impression on his attention. We see appear, in succession, the Shulamite in the midst of clouds of perfumes, the divan of Solomon escorted by sixty body guards, chosen men, marching with naked swords in their hands, and followed by the magnificent couch which has been provided for the ceremony. Only the spectators do not yet know who is to be the happy spouse, who is to partake of it, and imagine that it is to be, as formerly, a daughter of Jerusalem. At length the King appears himself, with the crown of the espousals upon his head. The mistake of the spectators, the pomp, the royal state, also indicate the royal residence, Jerusalem. That presumption is confirmed by the final call to the daughters of Sion, who are supposed to hasten forward, and who receive here their title of honour, while in the rest of the poem they are always called simply the daughters of Jerusalem.

CHORUS OF THE INHABITANTS OF JERUSALEM.

III. 6. Who is this that cometh out of the wilderness,
  Like pillars of smoke,
  Perfumed with myrrh and frankincense,
  And all kinds of sweet odours ?*

---

* The cortege appears to have been preceded by the *thurifers*, in the midst of whom proceeded the Shulamite, no doubt veiled (which explains the mistake of the spectators, verse 10), and seeming to be shrouded by the vapours which rose in columns round her. The espou-

7. Behold his bed, which is Solomon's,
Three score valiant men are about it,
Three score valiant men of Israel,*

sals are not yet completed, and this is merely a preparatory ceremony by which Solomon hopes to dazzle the girl and to render her agreeable to his wishes. It is interesting to compare with this, the description which Quintus Curtius gives us (viii. 9) of the manner in which the Indian kings proceed in public : " Servants," says he, " preceded, carrying " censers, and filling with perfumes the way by which the king was to " pass. The king himself reposed upon a litter of gold, adorned with " garlands of pearls. His clothes were of gold and purple." The first Book of Kings, ch. x. 22, mentions the trading by which Solomon increased the luxury of his Court.

* There is here, apparently, some contradiction of what we read in 2 Sam. xv. 18, xx. 7, and 1 Kings i. 38-44. According to these passages the body-guards of David and Solomon were strangers, Cherethites and Pelethites. The general opinion now is, that these names designated mercenary soldiers of Cretan and Philistine origin. Like other monarchs of the East, and even some European kings, the kings of Israel preferred foreigners to their own subjects for their personal body-guards. There is no more difficulty in understanding the King of Israel to be guarded by Philistines, than the Pope and the King of Naples being surrounded by Swiss, republicans and often Protestants. Elsewhere we learn that David had some devoted partizans in the Philistine district of Gath (2 Sam. xv. 18, &c.), and David himself was proposed as a body-guard to the Philistine king Achish (1 Sam. xxviii. 2, comp. xxvii. 12). Perhaps the apparent contradiction is resolved by the fact that the sentiment of repugnance with which the protection of their government by foreign soldiers is viewed in modern Europe, was unknown in Oriental antiquity, and that once incorporated into the royal army, the mercenaries became "valiant men of Israel" on the same footing as the others. It may be, in the same manner, that the Ephraimite author of the Canticle describes the women of the harem as "daughters of Jeru-" salem," although we know that the foreign element prevailed in it also. 1 Kings xi. 1.

8. They all hold swords, expert in war,
   Every man hath his sword upon his thigh,
   Because of fear in the night.
9. King Solomon made himself a bed,
   Of the trees of Lebanon.
10. The pillars thereof are of silver,
    The supports are of gold,
    The couch is of purple,
    In the midst thereof will shine his chosen one,
    Chosen among the daughters of Jerusalem.
11. Go forth, O ye daughters of Zion,
    And behold King Solomon,
    With the crown wherewith his mother crowned him,
    In the day of his espousals,
    And in the day of the gladness of his heart.

Solomon, without doubt, thought that her distance from her native place, and the pomps displayed around her would overcome the resolution of the girl. He recommences to praise, in most flattering terms, the attractions of the Shulamite. We refer to what we already said in regard to the language of Oriental gallantry. Besides the neck compared to the tower of David, the comparison of the teeth to a flock of sheep that are shorn, and come up from the washing, walking two and two together, corroborates our previous remarks. We ask permission to pass over the farther enumeration of feminine charms. It adds nothing to the development of the drama, and contains passages which can scarcely be rendered in a modern translation (ch. iv. 1-7). Let us remark, however, that verse 7 has taken position for several years among the passages which are cited in favour of the immaculate conception.

The Shulamite is unwilling to understand, in a disquieting sense, the words of verse 6. She snatches at the word *Lebona,* incense, which terminates it, and which, by the resemblance of sound recalls to her the mountains which she has more than once traversed with her shepherd. She connects then to that word a new song, a *solo,* similar to the first song of the preceding scene, and which, like it, depicts the love which she inspires to her betrothed. To the far-fetched compliments of the king, she opposes sentiments more vigorous, more true, and in reality more flattering, on behalf of the young mountaineer. The language is impassioned but it is more chaste than that of the king. The name which she, speaking as the lover, gives to her well-beloved is that of her betrothed sister. His language is delicious to her ear as milk and honey is to the palate. He compares her to a fresh garden, closed to every one, but filled with precious flowers, the perfumes of which are exhaled for himself alone. So the girl promises herself to him, and the song terminates by a sort of invocation (ch. v. 1), which the chorus delighted, no doubt, with this song of love, gives out in sign of sympathy.

FIRST SONG OF THE SHULAMITE.

IV. 8. Come with me from Lebanon, my betrothed,
   Come with me from Lebanon,
   Look from the top of Amanà,
   From the top of Shenir and Hermon,
   From the lions' dens,
   From the mountains of the leopards:
9. Thou hast ravished my heart, my betrothed sister,
   Thou hast ravished my heart with one of thy glances,
   With one of the circles of thy neck.
10. How fair is thy love, my betrothed sister,
    How much better is thy love than wine,
    And the smell of thine ointments than all spices,
11. Thy lips, O my betrothed, drop as the honeycomb,
    Honey and milk are under thy tongue,*
    And the smell of thy garments is as the smell of Lebanon.
12. Thou art a garden enclosed, my betrothed sister,
    A spring shut up, a fountain sealed.

* Theocritus (Idyll xx. 26, 27) presents a parallel resembling very much this manner of describing the inherent charm of the voice of a person beloved:

Το στομα και πακτας γλυκωτερον εκ στοματων δε
Ερρεε μοι φωνα γλυκωτερα η μελικηρω.

13. Thy plants are an orchard of pomegranates,
   With pleasant fruits, cypress and spikenard,
14. Spikenard and saffron, calamus and cinnamon,
   With all trees of frankincense.
   Myrrh and aloes, with all the chief spices.
15. A fountain of gardens, a well of living waters,
   And streams from Lebanon.
16. Awake, O north wind,
   And come, thou South,
   Blow upon my garden,
   That the spices thereof may flow out.
   Let my beloved come into his garden,
   And eat his pleasant fruits.

V. 1. I am come into my garden, my betrothed sister,
   I have gathered my myrrh with my spice,
   I have eaten my honeycomb with my honey,
   I have drunk my wine and my milk.

CHORUS.

Eat, O friends, drink,
Enrapture yourselves of love.

This indirect response to the king, ought to show him how much her lover knew better than him the way to her heart. But as in the preceding scene, the first *solo* is followed by a second which will develop, in its turn, the vivacity of the love which, on her side, she also bears to her betrothed. She does so, in relating a dream in which she believes that he knocks at her door. Under the impression of this dream, and after some objections on account of her alarmed modesty, she rises to open the door to him, but, of course, he was not there; and as she continues under the illusion, she searches and calls for him. The noise attracts the watchmen, who beat her, and remove her veil. But the result is, that, by night as well as by day, her soul is entirely devoted to her betrothed, and will not be so to any other.

SECOND SONG OF THE SHULAMITE.

V. 2. I sleep, but my heart waketh,
The voice of my well-beloved knocketh,
' Open to me, my sister, my love,
My dove, my undefiled,
My head is filled with dew,
And my locks with the drops of the night.'*

3. I have put off my clothes,
How shall I put them on?
I have washed my feet,
How shall I soil them?

4. My beloved put in his hand by the window,
And my heart was moved for him.

---

* This is a new trait of analogy with the songs and manners of the Arabs. "When a lover cannot sleep he goes to the part of the tent "reserved for men, or to a neighbouring tent belonging to a friend, and "sings his *Hodscheini* (a love song) in order to induce his fair one to "shew herself." Meier, from Burckhardt, p. 77).—May it not be inferred that the Spanish serenade is of Arabic origin?

5. I rose up to open to my beloved,
   And my hands dropped myrrh,*
   And my fingers sweet smelling myrrh,
   Upon the handles of the lock.
6. I opened to my beloved,
   But my beloved was not there,
   My soul failed me when he spake,
   I sought him but I could not find him,
   I called him, but he gave me no answer.
7. The watchmen who went about the town found me,
   They smote me, they wounded me,
   The keepers of the walls took away my veil from me.
8. I conjure you, O daughters of Jerusalem,
   If ye find my beloved,
   That ye tell him
   That I suffer from love.

We come here to a trait of great *finesse*. We have seen in the former scene that the women in whose company the Shulamite had been placed, obeyed superior orders, in exhorting her to accept the position which the king wished to give her, but were not very well disposed towards her. Now the poem indicates here a change in their disposition towards her, which

---

* Myrrh is here a symbol of the love which fills her whole being, so far that it drops from her fingers upon the door. It comes advantageously in place of what a romancer of the school of Balzac would probably describe as electric fluid, or as a magnetic current.

soon becomes true sympathy. They conclude from the impression of a love so strong and so true as to repulse the offers of King Solomon, that the object of it must possess exceptional merit, and in place of turning into derision, as they did on the former occasion, the inclination of the girl for a simple shepherd, they question her thus :—

CHORUS OF WOMEN.

9. What is thy beloved more than another beloved,
O thou fairest among women?
What is thy beloved more than another beloved,
That thus dost charge us so?

The Shulamite then describes the beauty of her lover (10-16), and this description is a pendant of that which King Solomon had made to herself of her own charms. She terminates by these words a sort of ingenuous pride :

16. Such is my well-beloved,
Such is my friend,
O daughters of Jerusalem.

The poet carefully avoids putting into the response of the women any words of doubt or mockery. Indeed, every woman who loves would have spoken in the same manner of her beloved, but the profound affection which her words express, affects the women themselves, as she idealizes the lover in the eyes of his betrothed. This is then the first victory achieved by the force of true love. The same women who at first scoffed at her pastoral amours are now softened, and join with the Shulamite in wishing that she may find her betrothed, and offer to aid her in doing so.

CHORUS OF WOMEN.

VI. 1. Where is thy beloved gone,
O, thou fairest among women,
Where is thy beloved gone,
That we may seek him with thee?

But the Shulamite cannot describe the pasturages where, since her being carried away, her betrothed now feeds his flock.

THE SHULAMITE.

2. My beloved is gone to his garden,
To the beds of spices,
To feed in the gardens,
And to gather lilies.
3. I am my beloved's,
And my beloved is mine,
He feedeth among the lilies.*

Scene 4. We still continue at Jerusalem, and the only thing which makes a change here, in the unfolding of the drama, is that the means of persuasion to which Solomon has recourse differ from those which he tried previously. He no longer tries to gain the girl merely by flattery and by dazzling her with

---

* Compare ch. ii. 16. This repetition also shows that nothing is changed in her inclination.

ostentation. He offers her the first place among his women, or, as it may be said, to make her his favourite sultana. This offer of the king is sustained by the homage which the poet describes the women themselves as rendering to the unrivalled beauty of the young Shulamite.

SOLOMON.

VI. 4. Thou art beautiful, O my love, as Tirzah,*
Comely as Jerusalem,
Terrible as an army with banners.†

5. Turn away thine eyes from me,
For they have overcome me.

*   *   *   *   *

8. There are threescore queens,‡
And fourscore concubines,
And virgins without number.

9. But one is my dove, my undefiled,
She is the only one of her mother,
She is the choice one of her that bare her.

---

* Tirzah is a town of Canaanite origin (Josh. xii. 24), and during some time it was the residence of the kings of Israel (1 Kings xiv. 17; xv. 21, 33; and xvi. 8). It is for that reason it is put here in parallel with Jerusalem.

† Solomon admits here that he feels himself deterred by the firmness of the Shulamite.

‡ This very considerable number of spouses mentioned in a passage, the object of which cannot be to diminish the renown ascribed to Solomon, suggests that there may be some legendary exaggeration in what is stated in 1 Kings xi. 3. But how has M. Delitzch, in the face of such passages, been able to imagine that the type of matrimonial purity, and of marriage as a divine institution, is represented in the Canticle?

The daughters saw her and blessed her,
The queens and the concubines praised her.

CHORUS OF WOMEN.

10. Who is she that looketh forth as the morning,
Fair as the moon,
Clear as the sun,
Terrible as an army with banners?

Then the Shulamite makes the king understand seriously that it is against her wish to go to his harem. Perhaps Solomon had suspected some interested motives when he learned that she was found wandering alone near the royal encampment. She declares to him distinctly, that it was in entire ignorance, and while thinking of her love, that she had so wandered.

THE SHULAMITE.

11. I went down unto the garden of nuts,
To see the fruits of the valley,
To see if the vine flourished,
If the pomegranates budded.*
12. I know not how my heart led me
Near the chariots of the nobles of my people.

Now comes a chorus which we scarcely know what to ascribe to. In my opinion, there does not appear to be any other admissible explanation than that which

---

* We see, in referring to ch. ii. 13, that the girl makes allusion to the promenade which her lover had proposed to her, and which she wished to make alone, not being able to enjoy his society.

puts it in the mouth of the people of Shulem, who lament the disappearance of their fair compatriot. She was the ornament of their *fêtes*. All eyes were fixed upon her when she danced. This intervention of the Shulamites is, no doubt, a perfect dramatic improbability, but it is full of grace in such popular poetry. There is nothing sweeter than some of the words of it, repeating themselves from the distant echo : " *Schouby, Schouby, ha Schoulamith, Schouby, Schouby,*" &c.

CHORUS OF SHULAMITES..

13. Return, return, O Shulamite,
Return, return, that we may look upon thee.
Why will ye look on the Shulamite
As the dance of Mahanaim ? *

VII. 1. How beautiful are thy feet
With shoes, O daughter of a noble.†

Perhaps, also, the Ephraimite poet wished to make it to be understood by that, that the compatriots of the girl would avenge her if she were detained

---

* Mahanaim was a great and ancient city of the north of Palestine (see 1 Sam. ii. 8; xvii. 24; xix. 32, &c.). An old myth connected itself with the name (Genesis xxxii. 1, 2), and probably the tradition led to some annual *fête*, or rejoicing, at which the surrounding population gathered themselves.

† Literally, daughter of a noble, or of a man free and well off, as that appears from the last song of the brothers (ch. viii. 8) to be the state of the fortune of the family. This strophe presents a new resemblance to the Arabic *Asamer*, where the young girls advance in turn, dancing before the young men, who praise in a loud voice their movements and their graces. (Meier, after Burckhardt, p. 75.)

against her pleasure in the royal harem. It also explains better, from his point of view, the determination which Solomon finishes by taking. But he is not yet resolved. He tries a last effort, praising with passion the attractions of his captive. It is always the same kind of comparisons, drawn from things the most precious, from flowers the most esteemed, from perfumes the most rare—all appearing to us wonderfully strange. Thus the eyes of the Shulamite are compared to the fish-pools of Heshbon. Probably the water of these pools was renowned for its transparence and purity. A king is held in the curls of her hair (ver. 4 and 5).

But the response of the Shulamite remains inexorable. She belongs to her well-beloved, and her only desire is to rejoin him, and to enjoy with him the sweetness of the Spring-time. The fruits of the garden—her lover has so called her (ch. iv. 12)—have been guarded for him. Yet here chastity of thought predominates over the ardour of the images. "Oh!" she exclaims, "that thou wert as my brother." Finally, the conjuration to the daughters of Jerusalem is repeated, for the last time, with a slight shade of difference from previous occasions.

THE SHULAMITE.

VII. 10. I am my beloved's,
And his desire is toward me.
11. Come, my beloved,
Let us go forth into the fields,
Let us repose upon the flowers of the cypress.

12. Let us get up early to the vineyards,
Let us see if the vines flourish,
If the tender grapes appear,
If the pomegranates bud forth;
There will I give thee my loves.
13. The mandrakes* give a perfume,
At our gates are all manner of pleasant fruits,
New and old, my well beloved,
I have laid them up for thee.

VIII. 1. O that thou wert as my brother,
Nourished upon the bosom of my mother,
I should find thee without,
I would embrace thee,
Yea! I should not be despised.
2. I would lead thee and bring thee
Into the house of my mother,
Thou should'st teach me to give thee to drink
Of spiced wine and the juice of the pomegranate.
3. His left hand should be under my head,
And his right hand should embrace me.
4. I conjure you, O daughters of Jerusalem,
Why do ye stir up, why provoke love
Before the heart so inclines?

---

* Mandragores, or Belladonna, which in Palestine, above all at the environs of Thabor and Carmel, grow in great abundance, and fill the air in spring with intense and even intoxicating perfumes. It is also a symbolical plant which plays a great part in the amorous language of the East. (See Winer Realwoerterbuch, art. Alraun.)

We think, with M. Hoekstra, that this change in the form of the conjuration, which becomes here a triumphant interrogation, ought to vindicate the victory achieved by the Shulamite. It is no more a supplication that she pronounces, it is a morality that she draws.

Scene V. We see now the return into the country of Shulem. The girl has again found her betrothed, and returns supported on his arm. The chorus of her compatriots announces her arrival, as that of the inhabitants of Jerusalem had sung her entry into the capital (ch. iii. 6); but the description is naturally much shorter.

CHORUS OF SHULAMITES.

VIII. 5. Who is this that cometh from the plain,
Leaning on her beloved?

The Shulamite sings then a last *solo*, which contains the thought of the entire poem. True love is stronger than all obstacles; it is a lightning from God; it is neither bought nor sold. This song is addressed to her well-beloved, who is beside her. The apple-tree was the symbol of true love (compare ch. ii. 3, 5). The girl recalls to him that she has conquered his heart under the apple-tree, that is to say, under the auspices of sincere and mutual affection. From this comes her unalterable fidelity and the strength of her attachment.

SONG OF THE SHULAMITE.

VIII. 5. Under the apple-tree I won thee,
There thy mother has betrothed thee,
There she that brought thee forth has betrothed thee.
6. Place me as a seal upon thy heart,
As a seal upon thine arm,
For love is strong as death,
Ardent affection is unyielding as the grave,
The flames thereof are flames of fire,
The lightnings of Jehovah.
7. Many waters cannot quench love,
Neither can the floods drown it,
If a man would offer all that he hath for love,
He would receive contempt upon contempt.

The brothers re-appear once more upon the scene, and interrupt the amorous melody with the same abruptness, the same originality of which we have seen a former specimen (ch. ii. 15). It is an indirect question which they address to their sister, in declaring what they intend to do with another sister still younger than she is. If, when she shall be of marriageable age, her virtue shall have resisted as a wall the seductions which may be held out to her, they shall give her fair and rich adornments. If, on the contrary, she betakes herself to light conduct, as a door which yields to the least pressure, they shall not give her anything but the ornament to which a door has right—a frame of wood, that is to say, something of small value. This rude language, from which a sort of coarse good humour gleams out, contains, according to their manner, the morality of the poem. The sentiment reflected from family honour pleads the same *thesis* as impassioned love.

THE BROTHERS.

VIII. 8. We have a sister,
      A little sister,
      Yet without breasts,
      What shall we do for our sister,
      In the day when she shall be spoken for?
  9. If she be as a wall,
      We will build upon her
      Battlements of silver,
      If she be as a door
      We will inclose her
      With boards of cedar.

The elder sister understands the allusion, and, with legitimate pride, she attests her firmness in the midst of the royal seductions. She has at length found peace, the king, on account of her perseverance, has permitted her to go away, and she relates her history under a parabolic form, comparing herself to a vineyard fallen into the power of Solomon, which he had entrusted to keepers, and the produce of which was very valuable.

THE SHULAMITE.

VIII. 10. I have been as a wall,
      And my breasts as towers,

    And I have been in his eyes
    As one that found favour.
 11. Solomon had a vineyard
    In Baal-hamon.*
    He entrusted it to the keepers,
    Every one offered for its fruits
    A thousand pieces of silver.
 12. My vineyard, which is mine, is before me,
    Guard thy silver, O Solomon,
    And leave two hundred pieces to the guardians.

There is some obscurity in the last verse. It may be perhaps an ironical adieu which the girl lanced from the distance at King Solomon. He had not drawn any profit from the vineyard that he had acquired, and he ought even to recompense the keepers to whom he had entrusted it, in giving them at least a fifth of the return which he expected from it. The Shulamite, on the contrary, has her vineyard, her lover, near her, and has no need to entrust it to any person.

Her betrothed then speaks as if to assert his entire confidence in her assurances of fidelity. He then prays her to let him and his friends hear some of her sweet songs, of which they were deprived by her absence.

---

* That appears to be the locality in which Solomon was when she was taken away. The king, no doubt, had made a spring excursion into these pleasant countries. Hence the curtains of the tents of Solomon (ch. i. 5) in the same manner as the reference to the tents of Kedar.

HER BETROTHED.

VIII. 13. Thou that dwellest in the gardens,
Friends hearken to thy voice,
Cause me to hear it.

And the girl satisfies his desire, in repeating the strophe which she sang the day on which she was carried off, when she hoped again to see her betrothed before night.

THE SHULAMITE.

14. Make haste, my beloved,
Be like a roe, or a young hart,
Upon the mountains of spices.

The Canticle then terminates naturally, by the peaceful reunion of the two lovers, and it is difficult to comprehend why so many critics have maintained the end of the poem to be lost. What would they have after that? Have we not come to the moment for which, from the first verse of the poem, the fair Shulamite has sighed so ardently?

IV.

We hope that those of our readers who have accompanied us attentively concur with us in the striking probability of the explanation which has been given. Some differences in detail do not affect the results which we are about to state.

In the first place, we merely express what is the most evident thing of all, that Solomon cannot be the author of such a poem. How can it be imagined that a king would set about singing in charming verse, with inimitable verve and freshness, his defeat by a young peasant, whom he could not persuade to become his wife? We may lay aside the idea as absurd. This negation of the traditional opinion as to the authorship of the book, which is sufficiently evident to any one who may admit even the general tenor of the observations we are about to make, is supported by other indications. Thus, the superscription of the book, "The Song of Songs, which is Solomon's," is clearly from another hand than that of the author. For it presents an important contrast of dialect with all the rest of the poem. The dialect of the North of Palestine joined the relative pronoun to the first word of the preposition following, and in doing so reduced the pronoun to a single letter. On the other hand, in the classical Hebrew of Judah, they used the whole word in order to express the relative, *ascher*. And it is that word which is found in the superscription, whilst from the one end of the poem to the other it is the northern usage which is constantly followed. This is almost already conclusive that the poem has come from the North, and that its actual title has been given to it in the South. But there is more. The Septuagint has given the title of the book, not as we have it, but as the "Song of Songs, namely, Solomon."* Now this superscription, going back to a form more ancient

---

* Ασμα ασματων ο εστι Σαλωμων.

than ours, expresses an actual truth. The Canticle should be called "Solomon," not from the name of its author, but from the name of the principal person who figures in it, in the same way as so many other biblical books, poems, romances, histories, and as they have always named dramas. We could adduce other details which the traditional opinion renders incomprehensible.

We desire now to form some inductions as to the time and circumstances in which the song has been composed.

It seems to us that there are sufficient indications to enable us to affirm that the Canticle is a production of the North of Palestine, of the Ephraimite kingdom of the ten tribes, and that the approximate date of its composition ought to be assigned to the reign of Jeroboam II. (825-784 B.C.)

The Palestine of the North appears in the history of the Israelites, as less accessible to spiritualism, and to religious puritanism, less in reaction against nature and natural life, than the Palestine of the South. It is there also that popular poesy seems to have taken the most lively flight. In the benediction of Jacob, (Genesis xlix. 1-27), a national song of Israel, and containing a characteristic of each tribe, the northern tribe of Naphtali has for itself poetic genius, "he giveth goodly words." This is the same country from which we have the patriotic song of Deborah, the charming apologue of Jehoram, the histories of Gideon, of Jephthah, where the poetic element holds so much place, the prophecies of Hosea, so warm in colour, the prophets who have not written, but of whom history attests the vigorous action upon the popular imagination, Elijah and Elisha, the legend of Jonah, &c. The poetry of the South is more pure, more chastened, and is the classical poetry of the nation. It is every where much more exclusively religious. The kind of poetry, such as the Canticle, seems therefore more natural in the kingdom of the north than in that of Judah. There it would have been either much more religious, if it had been composed among the faithful Jews, or much less moral if it had owed its origin to the idolatrous party. In the latter case, ill-regarded from the first by men of monotheistic faith, it would never have entered into the biblical canon, made up by the scribes of Judah. Besides, it is not in the kingdom of Judah that Solomon would have been represented in a light so little flattering to him. An influence sufficiently powerful, however indirect, over their own manners and customs, and a manner of living less subordinate to the pre-occupations of the temple, and to the royal state maintained in Judah, would have been necessary in order to make the triumph of pure over sensual love, a subject of popular song. It may be added that the beauties of nature in the North, in the country of the Lebanon, of marvellous fertility, rich in woods, prairies, running streams, better inspire bucolic poetry than the sandy and frequently rocky districts of the South.*

* See Winer, Realwoerterbuch. art. Galilea.

It has been maintained that the Canticle was a satire directed by the popular malice of the North against the person of Solomon, that it was the expression of the sentiments of aversion against the dynasty of David, of which the tribes of the North gave prompt proof after the death of his son. It is impossible for me to join in that opinion. Solomon, no doubt, has not a pleasant *role* in the Canticle, and here and there there is an evident indulgence of ironical intention at his expense. But, after all, he is not charged with any odious deed. His pomp, his polygamy, are matters of history, and are nowhere charged against him reprehensively. The morality of the drama may be reduced to this formula: True love is so strong that it resisted even Solomon; and surely such a formula as this is not fundamentally malevolent against him. His giving the girl her liberty is a fine trait of its kind, and responds to the wisdom of the monarch, which is no more attacked by the story of her carrying off, which precedes, than he has been in the general tradition of the Semitic East, by his moral and religious vagaries. It seems to me that, taking every thing into view, the author of the Canticle has not had any political *arrière-pensee*, and that he wished simply to sing of a subject which was pleasing to his muse, in profiting, perhaps, of a local tradition which might well have an historic foundation. But, on the other hand, it is necessary to recognise that, in the population among whom the poem had birth, and among whom it was sung, the person of Solomon was far from holding the prestige which he otherwise exercised. In a word, in the Canticle there is no direct opposition to Solomon, but there is indifference, and complete absence of any fascination before his glory. This also carries us towards the Palestine of the North. The South was always more Davidical.

To these considerations, of which none who have carefully studied the history of the Hebrew people can misunderstand the value, are joined the remarks furnished by the text itself. Thus, with the exception of Jerusalem and Engaddi, all the localities of which mention is made, Sharon, Gilead, Tirzah, the Lebanon, Amana, Hermon, Shenir, Carmel, Mahanaim, Baal-Hamon, the country of the heroine, appertain to the kingdom of the North. They see that the author knows the places, and that which distinguishes them. He has seen the goats of Gilead (ch. iv. 1), the tower of Lebanon which commands the road to Damascus (ch. vii. 4). He knows the fishpools of Heshbon, he knows that they are near the gates of the town, and he knows the names of the gates (ch. vii. 4). Some ruins, yet visible,* attest the exactitude of these indications. Tirzah is mentioned as a fair city (ch. vi. 4) which can be compared to Jerusalem. On the contrary, no detail of that kind indicates the same knowledge of the localities of the South.

Farther, the language is that of the North. We have already noticed the *schin* prefix, substituted everywhere to *ascher*. We could still adduce a suffi-

* Robinson's Palestine, 3, 924.

ciently long list of Aramean or Aramaic expressions which lead to the same conclusion. But we refer for them to the special treatises which we have cited.

What is, then, the period of the history of the Palestine of the North, which presents a favourable occasion for the nourishing of these delicate flowers of popular poesy?

It is inadmissible that the Canticle could have been composed after the destruction of the kingdom of the North. Its admission into the Biblical canon is entirely opposed to this. We are then limited to the period between the death of Solomon (975) and the invasion of Shalmaneser (721). For we can no longer suppose the composition of such a poem, during the lifetime of Solomon. Now, that period, however extended, presents scarcely but one moment when the appearance of the Canticle might be probable. It may be assumed that the idyll, the bucolic poesy, requires, in order to strike from its lyre sounds so sweet and fresh, a period of calm in which the people may give themselves up to their industry and rustic enjoyments. That was not when the Syrian devastated the country, when civil war unchained its furies, when the women hid themselves in the forests and mountains, and the young men were constantly under arms. It is not at such a time as that, that people gather together in the evenings to hear the singing of girls, and to celebrate with them the beauties of nature and the enjoyments of rural life. In such times, the cultivators of the fields can scarcely recognize or protect their own. Now, during the whole period between 975 and 721 (B.C.) I cannot see but the reign of Jeroboam II. (825—784) which gave to the kingdom of Israel any continuation, sufficiently long, of peaceful and prosperous years.* At the termination of a fortunate war against the Syrians, from whom he took the territories of Damascus and Hamath, he assured to his people a tranquil possession of their country, such as neither before nor after is to be found in the history of their kingdom. The manners of the Court became softened and refined under the influence of a luxury and prosperity without precedent. We can see this from the contemporary prophecy of Amos. (See ch. vi. 1 and following verses, particularly ver. 5.) After Jeroboam II.'s reign of forty years came the return of anarchy, of bloody revolutions, and continual wars with Syria and Assyria. At first, there might appear to be reason to draw back the date on account of the parallelism of Tirzah and Jerusalem (ch. vi. 4), as from the time of Omri (923—918) it was at Samaria that the kings of Israel resided. But the ancient capital might preserve the remains of her grandeur, and the author of the poem might very well know that, in the time of Solomon, there could be no question of Samaria as the rival of Jerusalem. If, at the time of the schism, the kings of Israel first fixed themselves at Tirzah, that must have been on account of its importance; and even long after the translation of their residence to Samaria, Tirzah was the seat of a conspiracy

---

* See 2 Kings xiv. 23, et seq.

against King Shallum. (2 Kings xv. 13, 14.) There was, perhaps, a proverbial parallelism of very ancient date between the two cities, and of a nature not to be modified by poetic usage. But that which decides me principally is that, before Jeroboam II., I cannot imagine the production of such a work as the Canticle under the troubles and wars which prevailed in the reigns of Nadab, Baasha, Elah, Omri, Ahab, Jehoram, Jehu, and Jehoahaz. The time that we indicate is also that at which the hatred against Solomon, which, of course, was strongest at the epoch of the separation, had given place to a certain degree of indifference. The Israelites' had had time to see that what they reproached so severely against the house of David was almost an inevitable consequence of royalty. It is a very curious fact which is brought into notice by M. Hoekstra, that the 45th Psalm, which is an epithalamium celebrating the nuptials of a Hebrew king, presents in its seventeen verses singular resemblances, both in substance and in form to the Canticle, and that there is no Israelite prince to whom the strophes of that psalm apply so well as to Jeroboam II.

We have now to explain the admission of such a book into the Biblical Canon.

It is often thought that the transportations in mass of the Israelite population, by order of their Asiatic conquerors, rendered absolutely desert the countries stricken by these terrible decrees. It ought to be kept in view that many things necessarily prevented the absolute accomplishment of such orders. There is always a part of the people condemned, who succeed in concealing themselves, above all in mountainous countries; and there are always villages, and even districts, which escape the attention of the conqueror. It is the fact that, after the destruction of the kingdom of Israel by Shalmaneser, and the transportation of the greater part of the inhabitants, there was, among the Israelites who escaped from that measure, a very natural reconciliation and gathering together with their brothers of Judah. King Hezekiah* promoted this with all his power, and tried to re-establish between the two branches of Israel the religious unity which had been so compromised since the schism. He even exercised tolerance towards the men of the north so far as to pardon, to those who entered into his views, several illegalities proceeding from their ignorance of the paschal law (2 Chron. xxx. 17—20), and shortly afterwards it is very astonishing to see (ch. xxxi. 1) the men of Israel animated with more lively zeal than many of the men of Judah against the groves and the high places. At verse 6 of the same chapter, express mention is made of the children of Israel who inhabited the cities of Judah. It resulted naturally from that mixture that the popular productions of northern poetry were known and vulgarised in the south.

The Song of Songs, that is to say, the Song *par excellence*, the most beautiful of songs, sufficiently merited its name of honour to become one of those most widely spread. It may be doubtful if, by that

---

* 2 Chron. xxx. and xxxi.

time, its whole bearing continued to be thoroughly understood, when it is considered how little the people of present times understand the songs of our ancestors, although they repeat them without changing a word. In other respects the local manners of Judah, more legal, more prosaic, more urbane, did not, like those of the north, favour these animated repetitions of the pastoral drama. The Canticle, which was infinitely pleasing, from its charming details, even when they might have lost the key to its general construction, presented nothing to them unfavourable to its moral reputation. Those who first sang it in Judah would certainly offer it as a moral song which celebrated the victory of chastity; and marriage was too sacred an institution in the national estimation of the Hebrews for them to doubt the moral propriety of describing the joys and rapture of the love which precedes it. It was only at a later epoch, after the captivity, and under the influence, at least indirect, of the Persian dualism, that the institution of marriage lost its religious value, of which we see the result in the doctrines of the Ebionites and the Essenes. In a word, the Canticle could acclimatize itself in the kingdom of Judah, with excellent estimation, even in the eyes of the faithful. It is after that, no doubt, that the tendency to allegorise it must have commenced. When it came to be no longer understood in its original application, when the order of things, the manners, the customs to which it made allusion had entirely disappeared, beyond the prospect of return, from the life of the Jewish people, the song itself continued to be handed down in the popular memory as a venerable one which their fathers had sung; and with the theocratic spirit, which prevailed at the period at which the Canon was formed, there was no more required to make them perceive, little by little, mysteries, types, and allegories in its poetic descriptions. The name of Solomon, which recurs in several parts of the poem; his renown, continually increasing, in the penumbra of the national tradition, for profound wisdom; the symbolic language of many prophets, who compared the alliance of Israel with God to a marriage, and its rupture, by the fault of the former, to an adultery, were the middle terms of which the re-union formed the bridge by which the Jews passed from the forgotten literal sense to the allegorical sense. The imagination once led in that direction, it was no more difficult to ascribe the Canticle to Solomon, who had himself been a poet and composed songs (1 Kings iv. 32), than to ascribe to him, as was done, without any more grounds, the whole collection of the Proverbs, and the book of Ecclesiastes.

To resume : the admission of the Canticle into the Canon has been preceded—1st, by the propagation in the kingdom of Judah of the Canticle brought along with them by the Ephraimite refugees under Hezekiah; 2nd, by the high reputation which it then held; and 3rd, by the tendency to allegorise in a theocratical-religious sense which, in the circumstances, became more easily applicable to that book than to any other.

We cannot close without saying some words upon

the position of modern interpretation in regard to this book. It has been very ill treated. It has suffered alike at the hands of its warmest admirers and of its 'detractors. This pearl of ancient poesy, of the finest water, and of the purest sparkle, has been equally misunderstood by both. Let us endeavour to pronounce upon it impartially, according to what we now know, without allowing ourselves to be blinded by ill-founded prejudices on the one hand, or by admiration still more unfounded on the other.

I admit that the book is not penetrated with the same religious spirit as the most of the other Biblical books. But it has nothing to fear, in that respect, in comparison with some fragments of the Book of Judges, or of the Proverbs, or with the Book of Esther. As to the fundamental idea with which it is inspired, it is not, in the view of a Protestant public, that it ought to be necessary to maintain its profound morality. The book speaks of love, of the ardent and passionate love of two betrothed persons towards each other. Well! it speaks of an institution of God, and if it speaks with more unreserve than is agreeable to our modern delicacy, it remains to be considered if we have much cause to glorify ourselves in that respect. I beg to make this reflection that, in France, we undergo, more than we are aware, the influence of the Roman Catholic atmosphere which surrounds us. It is very remarkable how much, in Protestant countries, the relations of the two sexes, their ideas of marriage, and of its normal conditions, differ from that which prevails among us. The farther you proceed into the regions of Southern Catholicism, the more that difference increases. This is not astonishing after all. In the doctrines of Catholicism the married state is an inferior one; the celibate, the perfect one. The model education is that of the convent or the clerical seminary, and the family is a *pis-aller*. I can understand that, to the eyes of the moral Catholic, the normal love of two individuals of different sexes, which is a sentiment as spontaneous in man, as much in accordance with his destiny, as paternal or filial love, has always something of the forbidden fruit.* There ought not to be the same among us; and those who persist in deploring the presence of the Canticle in the Bible, because it almost exclusively treats of love, sacrifice, without wishing to do so, to a Roman Catholic prejudice of much more remote origin than the Popes, and having its roots in the dualism of antiquity. It is in the Canticle as in the chaste nudities of statuary—to the pure all things are pure.

Do we then maintain the Canticle to be an edifying book? No, certainly not. It is no more so than a great many parts of the Old Testament which we can point out. But that its reading may be profoundly instructive; that it holds a remarkable place among the documents

---

* I hope that I express myself clearly. I am far from denying that there are some cases in which it is necessary to renounce a wife (actual or future) as there are others in which it is necessary to renounce a father, a mother, and children. Only I say that such cases should not be made to arise voluntarily.

of Hebraic antiquity; that it opens new perspectives of high interest upon the life and real manners of the people, of which we are apt to form a sort of official opinion little resembling the reality; that, in a word, it aids us better to understand that stem which increased, and from which ultimately the Gospel burst forth; and that, by all these claims, it occupies a legitimate place among the records of the old Covenant, we maintain firmly. For it is a false idea which refuses to accord to a book a place in the Bible, unless it be strictly religious. It is necessary to the historical value of the collection that this book should hold its place there.

We learn, for example, in reading this book, what does not directly flow from its religious interest, namely, how it took place that Solomon was the author of the ruin of his dynasty. In bringing foreign customs and ideas to the soil of Palestine, he greatly shocked the spirit and tendencies of the nation. Polygamy was not forbidden in Israel; but their manners tended naturally to monogamy, more especially in the rural districts. The pomp displayed by the king dazzled their judgment; but when it became necessary, in order to maintain it, to lay heavy imposts upon the rural population, the old instincts of independence and decentralization did their work. The religious syncretism to which he abandoned himself during the last part of his life, as a freethinker, who sacrificed under different symbols to the same Deity, was not only an anomaly, but, in addition, involved lesenationality at a time, and in a nation, in which the ideas of God and of country were so much blended together. Solomon, in place of developing the virtual powers of his people, the religious and moral tendencies inherent to their proper genius, wished to make them like other nations, without perceiving that Israel drew its grandeur precisely from the fact that it was not like other nations, and that in wishing to assimilate it to them, he reduced it to being inferior to them. In reality, the author of the Shulamite, as a faithful and ingenuous organ of the natural sentiments of his people, is more attached to the God of Israel than to the anointed of the Lord. In the most solemn moment of his poem, when he makes the gravest chords of his harp to resound, he comes to pronounce the name of a God, and that God is Jehovah:—

VIII. 6. For love is strong as death,
   Ardent affection is unyielding as the grave,
   The flames thereof are flames of fire
   Of the lightnings of Jehovah.

In this book, which speaks so much of pleasure, and which, at the first view, is so exclusively terrestrial, we do not find the least trace of either idolatry or polytheism. So true it is, that the natural and pure sentiments which make part of true humanity are in intimate harmony with religious truth. It is the too sensual king who abandons himself, so much the more easily, to the foreign religions, that they make pleasure one of the elements of their worship, while the heroes of the

Canticle are necessarily monotheist. It is not the fair and proud girl, who proclaims, with so much energy, her exclusive love for her betrothed, and who at the same time allows to be seen so much naive modesty, and so much real chastity, in her impassioned recitals, that would take part in the impurities of the worship of Baal and of Astarte. It is in that sense that it can be asserted that love, such as it is understood in modern times, could not have arisen, but in a monotheistic community. Is it not necessary that the two sexes be on a certain footing of equality before it can be developed? Is it not necessary that one and the same God has made both the one and the other? In the nations surrounding Israel, the nature ascribed to their Gods involved the two principles, male and female, and hence the obscenities which mingled in their worship. Their strange forms of sacrifice, under their revolting monstrosity, contain, nevertheless, the idea,—frightfully disfigured,—of the sacrifice of self. But true love is essentially monogamous, and consequently counteracts spontaneously the consequences, ascetic or indecent, (more near than is supposed) of dualism.

It is thus that we can understand that the idea of a sole Creator, maintained itself among the people of Israel against all that might conflict with it. Precisely because the Canticle is not a religious book, properly called, precisely because it has sprung even from the enjoyments and diversions of the people, it shews us how much monotheism was the foundation of the sentiments and the life of the Hebrew people, since these sentiments were strictly indigenous, and since the life was such as repelled foreign influences. Behold the residue of Israel that cannot perish! Behold the seven thousand who would not bend the knee before Baal! They are far from being saints in the Christian idea of the word. Their ideal involves infinitely more than ours, of material life. They estimate its enjoyments much more highly than we do, and they seek them without the least false shame. But they have the spirit of rectitude, which consists in adhering firmly to the duties of which they are conscious. And they are the depositaries and transmitters of that monotheistic religiosity, which contains, in germ, the pure morality with which it has pleased God to endow the Semitic race, more particularly the Abrahamides, and among the latter, above all, the Israelites.

The Canticle is then, in its own manner, one of the witnesses the best qualified, of that religious predestination, which, with the Bible, we call the election of the people of Israel, and in virtue of which it was in its bosom, and in its bosom only, that should be born the Founder of the definitive religion of humanity.

THE END.

www.ingramcontent.com/pod-product-compliance
Lightning Source LLC
Chambersburg PA
CBHW020332090426
42735CB00009B/1506